Title: From Zero to Success!

Author: Nick del Castillo

Nick del Castillo is also the author of:
"Virtues to Happiness" © 2016
"Notions on Emotions" © 2020
"The Seven Signs of Charisma" © 2021

Dedication: This book is dedicated to my friend Bill Sims.

CreateSpace, © 2017

Kindle Direct Publishing, 2nd Edition © 2024

Foreword: from "Virtues to Happiness" Chapter 31

"31. Success

What is success? ... Let's be realistic[,] for most people it means the acronym 'MFP' which stands for 1) Money 2) Fame and 3) Power. Most people think that 'MPF' will satisfy their life. If that's the case, then why are there so many people who possess these oftentimes times sad? Why are they in unstable relationships? ...Why do they destroy their minds and their bodies? ... Why are they so depressed? The list goes on… We often [] associate the word 'success' with 'accomplishment' or 'satisfaction.' What did one 'accomplish' if on the inside they are a disaster and can hardly control themselves? Where is the 'satisfaction' of living a life that is full of vice? The problem is that people see money, fame and power as ends and not as means. There is nothing wrong with having abundant wealth, being popular or having a position of influence, yet people need to wake up and see that all these qualities or states should be used for the good of the others. If not, corruption will set in and consume the person. People with 'MFP' have what I call 'relative success' or even 'temporal success.' Success is something that is long term and goes much deeper than mere positions or wealth. In the greater sense of the term, a successful person:

1) Uses the qualities or opportunities given to them in order to better themselves and to serve the others

2) Is one who sacrifices himself for the sake of a cause that is greater than himself

3) Acknowledges the truth about the world and themselves

4) Does good deeds without seeking honors or praise

People have to acknowledge the 'unsung' heroes of this world. For example, the mother that raises her children with great love and support is one of the greatest successes in life. No matter how rich, wise or talented someone may be, they cannot do anything worthwhile if what they do is not directed towards the good of the others. The street cleaner that day in and day out works hard and does not complain is more successful than the CEO that is lazy and arrogant. This is because the street cleaner is a greater example in his virtue and work ethic, which has a greater example for the others." ~ from "Virtues to Happiness" – Chapter 31

Table of Contents:

Chapter 1: Now I'm Unemployed

Chapter 2: Networking

Chapter 3: There is No Job for Me

Chapter 4: Excuses?

Chapter 5: Why Do I Need a Job?

Chapter 6: Intrinsic vs. Extrinsic Motivation

Chapter 7: Become Who You are Meant to Be

Chapter 8: Résumé & Interview

Chapter 9: Commute to Work and Time Use

Chapter 10: Dealing with Others at Work

Chapter 11: Fighting Off Distractions...

Chapter 12: A Happy Worker is a Healthy Worker

Chapter 13: Family and Work Balance

Chapter 14: Career Building vs. Comfort Seeking

Chapter 15: How Much Money Should I Make?

Chapter 16: Business Ethics 101: The Liars

Chapter 17: Lucky Breaks and Opportunities

Chapter 18: The Rubicon of Risks and Rewards

Chapter 19: When Should I Retire?

Chapter 20: Never Burn a Bridge

Chapter 21: Share the Wealth!

Chapter 1: Now I'm Unemployed

You are not unemployed; you are "in between opportunities." No one ever said that life was easy, and if they did, they are either lying or ignorant. As time goes on there are times when things do not turn out as expected. We may even experience a period of suffering and pain. One of the most stressful moments in one's career is unemployment. You may be starting out without a job, have quit, got fired or even laid off. In any case, and needless to say, it can be a very difficult time.   Whether you have a family or not, we should act and put ourselves in the shoes of a parent with a large and poor family. As soon as we are unemployed, we should start hitting the road and looking for a job like a jeweler in search of precious gems. Our 'full-time job' should be to get a full-time job. Time goes by deceptively fast... and so does our money. Watch our savings slip through our grasp faster than quicksand! Yes, you will be surprised to see how quickly our resources can vanish into thin air. When we are down it can be a psychological downer.

One depth leads to another...one fall leads another… We must have faith that things will get better. If you don't, then they really won't. Let's be realistic, there are no guaranteed successes in life, but by being positive and optimistic you are on the right path to make a turn around. Don't fall into the trap that you can't because you feel you can't, or others say that you can't. You must silence all the negativity and focus on what's on your plate and the road ahead. We must learn from the past, be inspired by the future and live in the present. You can and you absolutely must. There is no other way.

Chapter 2: Networking

Yes, networking is important. If you have no clients, then you have no business. What would you say of a teacher without students? A motivational speaker without an audience? A mentor without mentees? In a mystical way, we are all dependent on each other. This is true directly and even indirectly since our society is like one giant family. When society does positive things, it affects everybody else positively and the reverse is true. When a sister or a brother goes astray, it affects everybody else. Some misconceptions in networking are in the following: "I need to network so that I can …

1) …get a better job."

2) …get a recommendation."

3) ...advance my career."

4) ...use the contact to get other contacts."

The problem with the four misconceptions just mentioned is not that they are bad in themselves, but they all can be very self-centered. Being this way makes you a more miserable person. In order to network effectively, you must have:

1) A genuine interest in the other person

2) Not think what I can get, but rather what I can give

3) Have the humility to accept being helped

4) Have the courage to help the others

In all the points discussed it doesn't mean that you will need to spend all your time with them or be their best friend per se, but rather never to use people to get ahead or to impress them. Even when we do have the chance to hobnob with the rich and famous we need to be the same person as if we were to converse with a poor stranger on the street. If possible, why network with the more influential people? The reason being that whatever industry we are in, we can always raise the bar in …

1) The Advancement of the Industry and

2) Improving the Ethical Tone of the Place.

Someone who has more experience and prestige can create a larger impact by virtue of their position than someone who is just starting out. It doesn't mean in any way that the person at the bottom is worse than the person on top, but if we are to change an industry for the better, the people with more experience have more of the human means to do so. True networking is about how you and your contact can help each other and if possible, to improve the world.

Chapter 3: There is No Job for Me

Aristotle said, "where your talents and the needs of the world cross: there lies your vocation." If you think about it, everybody has talents. Sure, some more than others, but everyone has some talent, that is something they can bring to the table. Whether it is small or large, it doesn't matter. Everybody can contribute to the benefit of themselves and the world through their work. Some reasons why we can't find jobs we like are in the following:

1) We are too lazy to look for them

2) We don't know what our talents are

3) We think we would not like certain jobs when in fact we might

4) We lack self-knowledge

5) We haven't developed our skills

6) Special circumstances or things beyond our control

Regardless of whether we like our work or not there is always something we can contribute. Sometimes it requires that we tough it out and in doing so you gain in:

1) Self-knowledge

2) Develop skills

3) Earn while you learn new things

4) Buy time to find what you really want

Chapter 4: Excuses?

Excuses? No, not for you! Excuses are like dirty laundry. We all have them and they all stink! Come on, turn the page and on to the next chapter!

Chapter 5: Why Do I Need a Job?

What if I am already wealthy and have no need for a job? I hit the lotto, got an inheritance, etc. ... That is a good point. Why go through the drudgery of everyday work if I can avoid it? Is not money the 'sole' purpose for work? Given a profound philosophical notion of mankind (women and men), we are only satisfied when we foster the growth of our love. It can be argued that we can grow in love when we work and even more so when we work well and with a noble purpose. If we were to stop working today will our level of happiness skyrocket? Probably superficially and briefly if that, but no matter what, in this life there are no shortcuts to happiness. Happiness comes from the giving of ourselves, not from more money or the passive pleasures that it may bring. A person that can sleep for half the day and chill out in the second half will never be happy, because of the emptiness in not having given of one's talents creates a void that can only be filled with the gift of self.

Do not get me wrong, there is nothing wrong with retiring from your job when the time is right, but retirement should not be a period of 'doing nothing' but more the attitude of 'let's do something different.' That 'something different' can be volunteering for a non-profit, helping the sick or the elderly, or even pursuing a creative hobby. We may not all be financial experts, but think about it, whatever we do, we want to achieve some good. We consciously or subconsciously are looking for a return on our investments. For example, in seeking out to be pleased or entertained throughout your life you are spending time in order to feel good, but that investment in excess can be detrimental since the long-term effects are empty results. If you invest in doing something productive then it may be challenging, but in the long run you will reap the benefits. The joy and

satisfaction of having used your time well is good, but

having used it for the benefit of others is even greater.

<u>Chapter 6</u>: Intrinsic vs. Extrinsic Motivation

What motivates a person can be a bit of a mystery. Some people go crazy and will do anything to win in a simple board game whereas others won't care if they win or lose in real life when there is a lot more at stake. Although there are many types of motivations there are two fundamental ones that you can have when at your job: to work out of necessity or because you have genuine interest. In a nutshell, intrinsic motivation is doing something 'because you want to' and extrinsic motivation is doing something 'because you have to.' Extrinsic motivation does not necessarily have to be something negative. For example, to be extrinsically motivated at your job to support your wife and kids is one of the noblest vocations. Many people would prefer a different job but know that to support their family they need the job they have. Even though it may not be the ideal situation, the good of supporting a family far outweighs the burden of a tough job. Ideally most people would like to be intrinsically motivated, but in reality, there is no perfect job. Even for people with dream jobs, which is apparently 'everything they ever wanted' there may be some tasks of the job that are necessary, but unpleasant. There may be days that are rough and even there may be circumstances beyond one's control that cause the job to go sour. A person who is in the same job for 40 years did not have every day go smoothly. As juxtaposed, as intrinsic and extrinsic motivations may seem, there is a paradoxical link between the two. For example, if you really want your dream job, but do not have the qualifications or means to achieve it, then you may need an extrinsically motivating job to get the intrinsically motivating one.

Chapter 7: Become Who You are Meant to Be

'Become who I am meant to be' what is that supposed to mean? What do I have to become exactly? If we look at the nature of things, there seems to be a correlation with structure and function. We know how animals use their abilities for survival whether it is the chameleon's camouflage in disguising itself from its enemies or the expansion technique of the blowfish to scare away its predators. Knowing what our talents are can be somewhat of a challenge, but with a little time and effort, people will discover their strengths and weaknesses. Even more difficult for us human beings is to know the end purpose of these talents. People have different opinions, but time and again people are happiest when they make the gift of self and in serving the others. So, in becoming what you are, do not get

20

sidetracked on what you want to be, but rather what you have, and what you can do to the best of your abilities to help yourself and the others. These vary depending on our circumstances, talents, opportunities, and health, but regardless of the conditions there is always something we can do and most of the time it is manifested in and through our day-to-day work.

Chapter 8: Résumé & Interview

Most people learn from what they see. Given our human nature we like tangible evidence, and when we cannot get this type of proof, we want to quantify it and particularly in that of success. Our résumé is not just a piece of paper with your accomplishments but also a reflection of you. If you have a stellar résumé, but have awkward spacing or misspelled words, that speaks for itself. In résumé managers are more impressed with what has been accomplished rather than adjectives that describe themselves. 'I organized a fundraiser with 1,000 attendees' sounds a lot more convincing than 'I am a good fundraiser that is responsible.' They want to know the 'what' and the 'how' not just the 'what'.

A CEO once told an interviewee: "In an interview I do not look for résumés, but the vibes that I get from the person." Yes, as you probably already know we often communicate more through our body language than what we have to say. Can 'what is on paper' match 'what is in person'? At the end of the day employers want three questions answered favorably.

1) Can you do the job? (Competence)

2) Can I trust you? (Reliability & Likeability)

3) How long will you stay? (Loyalty)

If these get answered favorably then they may communicate more to the interviewer than hundreds of brilliant on paper accomplishments. When on an interview, "challenge" the interviewer. Go for what you want and be honest about it because if you are not, then it will come back to haunt you with the following monsters:

1) Part 'X' of my job is unbearable or

2) I should have told them I can't stand doing 'Y'

In the interview, if you are candid, clear, and concise you will be more convincing to the interviewer.

Chapter 9: Commute to Work and Time Use

If you do not commute to work you must be responsible with how you use your 'extra' time. Sometimes we think it's great if we have a short or even no commute at all, but it comes at a cost since we need to have the discipline to use that additional time well. If you commute, use it productively. If you have a long commute, use it even more productively. We all know that time is super limited. We say we don't have time, but we do. What this should mean is that we have allocated all our time hopefully for the greatest priorities in our life. Whether it is our faith, family, studies, volunteering etc.... once again, we do have time, we just don't have time to waste. If you have set goals in life, then wasting just a few seconds on something stupid or frivolous is greatly abhorred. However, the funny part about all this is that if we spend three hours helping a friend or family member who is in need then the time lost is no time 'lost' at all. Every second was well worth the effort.

Chapter 10: Dealing with Others at Work

There is no perfect job, and there are no perfect coworkers. Being in a job with a coworker that is nasty, lazy or incompetent can really lower the tone of a work environment and sap one's energy. There isn't an exact science on how to handle difficult colleagues, but there are some general principles to keep in mind.

1) Try to understand what it is like to be in their shoes and to be sympathetic towards their circumstances.

2) Make an effort to be courteous, professional and friendly. If that is not reciprocated, then keep your conversations to a minimum, but find small opportunities throughout the day to show that you are not an enemy, but simply a coworker that desires the good of everyone in the workplace.

3) Pick your battles. It may not be efficient or even effective to snap at your coworker each time they drop the ball or make a mess, but there are certain times that are appropriate to correct your coworker when you have been offended or if they have done something egregious. When correcting, it should always be concise and done with clarity and charity. If your coworker sees that you are correcting a fault for the greater good of the person and not out of anger, then there is a greater chance that the coworker will be more accepting of the correction.

4) Beyond repair? Yes, there are times when it can be detrimental to stay with a rotten team member and in some cases, it may be best to move on. Even though this may happen it's best to see this as an option of last resort.

Chapter 11: Fighting Off Distractions...

We all get sidetracked at one point or another, sometimes even several times a day. Even though it is inevitable, we can all do a better job of catching ourselves when we notice that we are wandering off. The first step is identifying the source of our distractions which consist of the following:

1) The Material World: Smartphone, the Internet, and technology in general

2) Others: Your coworkers

3) Yourself: Your own imagination, memories and worries

Whether the distractions come from the outside or from the inside ultimately, we are to blame. It's an old saying, but 'we are our own worst enemy.' If we give in to distractions, guess what... we 'opened the door when someone was knocking.' We heard the 'knock,' but we did not need to 'open the door.' Although it can be difficult to stay focused, we have the capacity to choose our path. We are the designers of our own destiny when it comes to making decisions. Who can crack your will? If the temptation is strong, we must remain calm and fight for just a few moments or at least enough time to distract ourselves and we are now back on track. If the distraction is from the others, we must learn to minimize the distraction and get back to work, but be courteous. When we need to be assertive, we should disagree without being disagreeable. If we notice that we are distracted, let's return to our focus immediately. Giving in just a little bit can lead to a bad habit of wasting time repeatedly until we get used to it. Keep in mind that some distractions are seductive. If you click on one link it can lead to clicking on another and another. It is so easy to go deeper and deeper into the rabbit hole. Once you give in just a little, soon it's game over. Distractions are like door-to-door salesmen. Once they get their foot in the door it makes it all the more difficult for them to get out. So, it's better to stop them before the snowball effect takes place. If you are uncomfortable with something at work, it's better to let the 'cat out of the bag' and to speak up now, before things get worse. Although we do not know the future, we can mentally project how some things will turn out. If we are honest with ourselves, we will be able to stop potentially large problems. As Benjamin Franklin once said: "An ounce of prevention is worth a pound of cure."

Chapter 12: A Happy Worker is a Healthy Worker

It's common sense, but if you don't take care of your health, it will limit your productivity. If we want to be 100% at work we need to eat a well-balanced diet, get adequate sleep and exercise. Health is one of those things that if you let it slip by it will take a toll on your work and in your life in general. The following comments are mere opinion, but they may be of help.

1) Get Enough Sleep: Ben Franklin said: "Early to bed, early to rise, keeps a man healthy, wealthy and wise." Talk to all the big shots, there is something about waking up early that really makes a difference. Some advantages are in using the time to pray, exercise, plan your day, etc. simply to get your day off to a good start. This may be also a psychological boost as Aristotle said: "Well begun is half done."

2) <u>Eat Healthy Food</u>: There is some truth to the saying "You are what you eat." If you put in healthy nutrients, you will have a healthy body. If you eat junk, you will eventually feel like junk. It goes for anything in life. If you put in the effort, you will get good results. If you put in a poor effort, you will get poor results.

3) <u>Exercise</u>: We all need it. Even just getting your heart rate up for 20 - 30 minutes at least once a week is a healthy habit. Energy breeds energy. Exercise will keep you in shape and give you more energy. Work can sometimes be very stressful and exercise is a good biological and psychological antidote for conquering stress and getting your mind off the negativity that may have accumulated throughout your day.

Chapter 13: Family and Work Balance

There was a guest speaker who was a former CEO with a family that asked: 'What is the percentage of time that one should dedicate to work versus that of your family?' The audience was probably curiously pondering what it was? 60/40, 30/70 etc... To stun his audience, he divulged the percentages of 100/100! Although this is mathematically impossible, life is beyond math. He went on to say something to the effect that when you got married you did not say to your wife, I give you my 33% or even my 51%. When at work we should also give our 100%. No ambitious employer would accept anything less in an interview. Who says, 'I plan on giving my 49%?!' when 100% is sometimes not good enough. The question was not answered, but in a way, it was since you cannot apply a mathematical formula or scientific rule when family and work take precedence.

The family is our first institution. It is where we first learn

everything and it's normally where we are first loved. Our

coworkers, on the other hand, are there in particular jobs.

Most times, as people switch jobs they do not stay in contact

with all their former coworkers, yet often there should be a

continuity of going back to the family in every epoch of our

lives. If we do not, then we need to re-examine the priorities

in our lives and hit the reset button. Although you may

spend more time with your coworkers, spending time with

your family is more important.

<u>Chapter 14</u>: Career Building vs. Comfort Seeking

In life nothing is ever perfect. Even if you have your dream job there are tiny nooks and crannies in your day-to-day tasks that you either find unpleasant or difficult. Sometimes people hop from job to job to find the 'perfect fit' like an odd figure trying to fit inside a cookie cutter shaped hole. There is absolutely nothing wrong in seeking out a greater job or in attempting to advance your career by climbing the proverbial totem pole, but escaping from one job to another is sometimes counterproductive. You do not want to fall into the 'eternal' spiral. Consider these scenarios:

<u>Job #1</u>: 'I'm tired of a long commute...'

<u>Job #2</u>: 'These coworkers are so stubborn; I can get anything done...'

Job #3: 'This job is so boring, it's not what the ad said it would be in the job description...'

Job #4: 'This job is way too stressful...'

Job #5: 'My boss is the absolute worst that I have ever had! ...'

Job #6: 'This job is fine, but I can't go very long with this low pay and poor benefits....'

Jobs to infinity! The list goes on...

The way to break the perpetual chain of negativities is to focus on the positive. Go for a new job because you honestly think it's the best way to go and not because your back is against the wall. There are certain times when you are in an objectively negative situation that merits an exit, but oftentimes we can find an alternative to cope with the stress of work. There is a humorous adage that goes "Wherever you go, there you are." It sounds ridiculous since it is an obvious statement, but it can also be very profound.

If you have a negative attitude in your job, guess what? You will most likely have a negative attitude in the next one. On the other hand, if you are a positive person, you carry that wherever you go. Hence the adage: "Wherever you go, there you are!"

Chapter 15: How Much Money Should I Make?

In this life, the human heart will always have insatiable desires. If you make $50K per year you may soon want to make six-figures, once you hit that mark you wonder if you can become a millionaire and then realize that being a millionaire is not that impressive and now aspire to become a billionaire. Even if you are a billionaire there is no guarantee in the satiation of your desires. Nothing is ever enough. You want more and more. Is there something wrong with wanting to be rich? Is it being greedy to want to make more money?

In very simple terms there is nothing wrong with wanting to or in having more money, so long as you use it for the good and understand its relative importance. Think about it, if you have the capacity, fortune or the opportunity to make a ton of money then great, but keep these questions in mind:

1) Will the money come at the cost of what I value most?

2) Given my goals, is making more money really worth my time and energy?

3) Will the world and myself be better off if I pursue this wealth?

4) Will I be able to use it for the good?

5) Is my motivation for this pursuit noble and just?

Sometimes we need to ask for a raise or simply work a second job since there is the greater good of supporting your family. Other times working extra can be detrimental to you and your family. If you have an absent parent, the consequences of that absence can create far greater harm. Unfortunately, that damage is something that money cannot repair. Money and power are like magnifying glasses. Who we are now is the same who we will be with more money, the only difference is that when this giant 'magnifying glass' is drawn out in front of us then the following phenomenon will occur: If we are generous, it will be magnified into greater generosity. If you are selfish, then that will be magnified into greater selfishness.

<u>Chapter 16</u>: Business Ethics 101 - The Liars

Business ethics begins with the person. It is not companies that sell products and provide services, it's people that do. Business ethics boils down to the virtues of honesty and justice. The fundamental foundation in business ethics is honesty. Without honesty and trust business cannot get done. Liars hurt business. If this is true, then who are the liars? ...You and I are the liars. We all have lied at some point in our lives. There are different forms of lying, but they are all lies, nonetheless. People who are liars get bad press, it's seen as scandalous, and no one likes them. If this is the case, then why do we lie and particularly in the workplace?

1) <u>Fear</u> - We are afraid of getting fired.

2) <u>Humiliation</u> - We don't want to look stupid or be humiliated.

3) <u>Money</u> - We want more money.

4) <u>Prestige</u> - We want to get ahead.

I would venture to say that most of our coworkers, managers and bosses are not bad people. Although there really do exist some people that may desire our demise, most people are a mix of possessing noble qualities, but also struggle with their vices to one degree or another. Whenever we are asked to lie, we should not fall into this trap.

"Shouldn't we lie? After all, we can get away with so much and get what we want."

It seems to be the case, but it's bogus. Here's why.

1) If we lie, we create barriers between our coworkers, our clients and even ourselves. We are basically saying 'you are not worthy of the truth.' It breaks the universal bond of

unconditional love that people desperately seek out whether consciously or unconsciously in their relationships, families, friendships and even in the workplace. If you lie you are saying by your actions: 'I simply don't trust you.'

2) If you lie, you might get some business in the short run, but then you will eventually lose and burn out. If you are truthful, you may hurt some people and lose clients, but will get more business in the long run since people like to do business with people they can trust. Savvy business professionals know that you cannot put a price tag to trustworthiness and reliability. Just as a four-leaf clover is hard to find, so is an honest worker. When you find that person, the value to the business is paramount.

3) One lie leads to another. If you develop the habit of lying, it can be very difficult to stop. One evil deed can lead to another.

4) Liars and cheaters get caught. You cannot hide your virtues and vices. People will eventually figure it out. Just like a zebra can't hide its stripes neither can man hide from his true self. Even if you never get caught, lying makes you complicated since you get confused between truth and falsehood. You may ask yourself: 'Is this about truth or appearances?' and will not know the answer.

"What if I can close a huge business deal with just one small lie? Isn't it worth it to make billions and billions of dollars? I can donate most or even all of it to charities. The good of helping millions of people will far outweigh the evil of a little innocuous lie. After all, doesn't the end justify the means in this case, and isn't this the greater good?" First is the quick and punchy answer. The second is more explanatory:

1) The answer is NO.

2) Let's explore this in a deeper manner. In order to give an

exegetical answer, you need to understand the true nature of the human person and his or her teleology (i.e. the goal or end of mankind).

If I scratch a paper cup no one would be scandalized after all those items are disposable and of relatively little value in the grand scheme of things. However, if I scratch a masterpiece painting made by a renowned Renaissance artist the world would be scandalized and upset, but why? Both are material objects. Is the fact that someone from several centuries ago put more effort into making the item more valuable? Just because people acknowledge its scarcity, now it's worth millions of dollars. Really? What about a human being? How much is human life worth? No one in his right mind would ever place a price tag on a human person. Common sense will tell us that. If the final cause of the paper cup is the transfer of a liquid, and the final cause of a painting is admiration, what is the final cause of mankind?

... It's happiness, and this comes from having lived righteously. If scratching a paper cup is bad, scratching a painting is far worse, then what about "scratching" the soul of a human being? Paraphrasing the medieval philosopher St. Thomas Aquinas, he said that the moral good of one person is greater than the good of the entire material world. If telling a lie is of grave matter to the human being and affects the person's final cause (which is happiness) then all the money and power will not suffice for its proper teleology since both money and power are mere means and do not constitute or even contribute to the proper end goal of the human person. There are some things in life that are priceless. Why give up that which is priceless for something with a limited value? Any businessman would say that it's a poor investment. So, the ends do not justify the means. You cannot do something unethical to do something good. It's a moral contradiction. The good of the person is far greater than any material gain. At the end of the day, we should be honest, but develop social tact, and a knack for business skills. There are times when we must be blunt, but most times we can use our words to amicably disagree. If we are honest, we may be hurt, misunderstood or even dishonored but we will have done the right thing for the business, the others and for ourselves.

Chapter 17: Lucky breaks and Opportunities

Jobs are like sports. Particularly like football. You may have been able to march down the field for 91 yards and think you are doing so well... and then oops! You fumbled the ball and didn't make it to the end zone. You didn't go the whole 9 yards! ... On the other hand, you may be down on your luck and suddenly the football lands on your hands and can turn things around unexpectedly. Notice the key word 'unexpectedly.' Maybe there is a pop quiz, a pothole on the road or a creepy crawler in your room, but no reason to be perturbed. There is a notable ebb and flow in getting "good" and "bad" luck. At work, everything may be going poorly, sales may be down, you have a nasty coworker and an even nastier boss, and the office coffee tastes stale, yet you never know what the future may hold.

49

The key is to take advantage of opportunities and to overcome obstacles. 95% of a person's success lies in their character and drive, whereas the other 5% is in their intelligence and skills. After all, success breeds confidence. A new account could spark the next business boom. That coworker may move on to a new job and your boss may have a change of heart. Yes, at the office there might even be a new blend of coffee. We need to have the emotional intelligence not to flip out on 4th and long and to not rest on our laurels on 1st and goal.

Chapter 18: The Rubicon of Risks and Rewards

Why risk it when you can play it safe? Why play it safe when you can win? Aristotle described that each virtue at its extremes has an excess and a deficiency. For example, bravery is the virtue that is in between the extremes of foolhardiness and cowardice. Never taking any risks is ironically too risky since it can stunt your development and in not taking any risks you are taking the risk of missing out in helping yourself and the others. That is like having a great treasure, burying it, and living the rest of your life not spending a nickel nor investing it. This would be the equivalent of not having it at all. On the other hand, taking too many risks that are foolhardy, as we know, can have devastating consequences. Investing your life savings in volatile commodities can be too risky. The money on the graphs move up and down faster than a wild roller coaster. You can lose it all in the blink of an eye... So, when should we take risks and especially with jobs or even in our careers? Yes, like in many things there are no clear-cut answers but, in a nutshell, we should take what are called Calculated Risks. Here is some food for thought:

1) Think of the worst-case scenario... Got it. Now that you know what it is, are you willing to accept the potential consequences?

2) Is this a necessary risk or can it be avoided?

3) Is the good that can be gained far greater than the bad that can be experienced if it fails?

4) Have you studied the matter thoroughly? (know yourself, know the others, know your environment)

5) Do I have my back against the wall? (i.e. the last arrow in my quiver, the final shot before the buzzer?)

To sum it up, in the concept of Calculated Risks there are

two types to consider:

Scenario 1: I have "no choice" since not acting will result by default, in automatic failure or in a greater negative consequence which is inevitable.

Scenario 2: I do not have to take the risk, but I will to gain a greater perceived good. I understand and accept the consequences of complete failure.

The first scenario is almost obvious that we should take, yet, not everyone does due to fear or anxiety. Not taking this risk is deciding to fail. The second scenario is not so cut and dry. There are some gray areas. In those cases, we should use our best judgment. In our life of work some questions below may come to mind:

1) Should I switch jobs?

2) Should I ask for a raise?

3) Should I stay late at work?

4) Should I spend more time at home?

5) Should I start a new career?

Chapter 19: When Should I Retire?

Many people see retirement as the "light at the end of the tunnel." Once they are retired, they can live in peace and take it easy. Time and again no matter what, people are never satisfied and happy regardless of what they receive. Those that have tried to make their own utopia by escaping from their day-to-day realities and have gone on a quest for their own pleasures have failed miserably. At the same time with that mentality, you will become bored and sapped of life very quickly. On the other hand, those that retire with a specific goal or purpose in using their talents via a positive outlet have always been happy. Whether someone retires at 40, 60 or 80 is not really the point, but rather in their intentions, circumstances, and attitude. I like to see retirement not as a time to veg out, but a time to shift gears and to focus on other things.

Chapter 20: Never Burn a Bridge

Not everything in business will go smoothly. Sometimes relationships go sour, or things happen which may cause conflicts. In either case, we should 'never burn a bridge.' Even though we may no longer continue at a particular company we should always try to end on good terms. If we do not, we run the risk of leaving a 'bad taste in our mouth.' This metaphor is fitting since after you have eaten something and digested the food it has been broken down and gone. However, sometimes the flavors of the food consumed remain in your mouth for an extended period of time. Not parting on good terms can sometimes leave bitterness inside of you, which can be hard to get rid of. Even though people may have hurt you, it is best to forgive and to move on. You will be a greater person in doing so.

People generally have sensitive egos. We all live in glass houses, and we all throw stones. Even though others may hurt us, let's not return the negativity, but take the high road and be positive. Yes, always.

Chapter 21: Share the Wealth!

We have been given talents: talents that are different, talents that are unique, talents that are extraordinary, talents that are practical. …Whatever talent you have, share it with the others, let your brilliance shine like the sun and glitter like the stars. No talent is too small, and no talent is too large. Expand your spiritual container with generosity and fill it. If you are super thirsty, are you going to fill your glass halfway or to the brim? We need to be generous to the brim and even just a bit more, just above the surface of the water creating a semi-circle over the edge, before spilling over. If not, then we have to ask ourselves: What is the purpose of our work? Why am I here? In our jobs, and our careers let us look beyond the material world and simply strive to do good work at the service of the others and we will be happy!

www.ingramcontent.com/pod-product-compliance
Lightning Source LLC
Chambersburg PA
CBHW071803200526
45167CB00017B/1303